I0486002

Adult Coloring Book

De-stress and Relax

With Coloring

30 different patterns of mandalas,

paisleys and stained glass

Joan Ali

Copyright 2015

All Rights Reserved

Joan Ali

This Book Belongs To

. . . .

Phone. . . . .

Gone are the days when coloring were just for kids. Today even adults find coloring therapeutic. Coloring help you distress from a hectic day, help to relieve anxiety, tension and depression. You can also feel calm and connected to yourself. Some people even color to relieve their headaches and minor pain.

So set some quiet time aside and take out your coloring book, crayons, markers or colored pencils and start coloring. Remember you are coloring for yourself so choose any color that you feel connected to at the time of coloring and you can start on any page.

If you have small children ask a family member if they can watch the children for an hour or so for you.

There are several mandalas, paisleys and stained glass and other patterns to color. The other side of the page has been left blank except for inspirational quotes in case there is any bleed from coloring the picture.

This book will make great gifts for family members, friends and co-workers.

Relax and Have Fun!!!

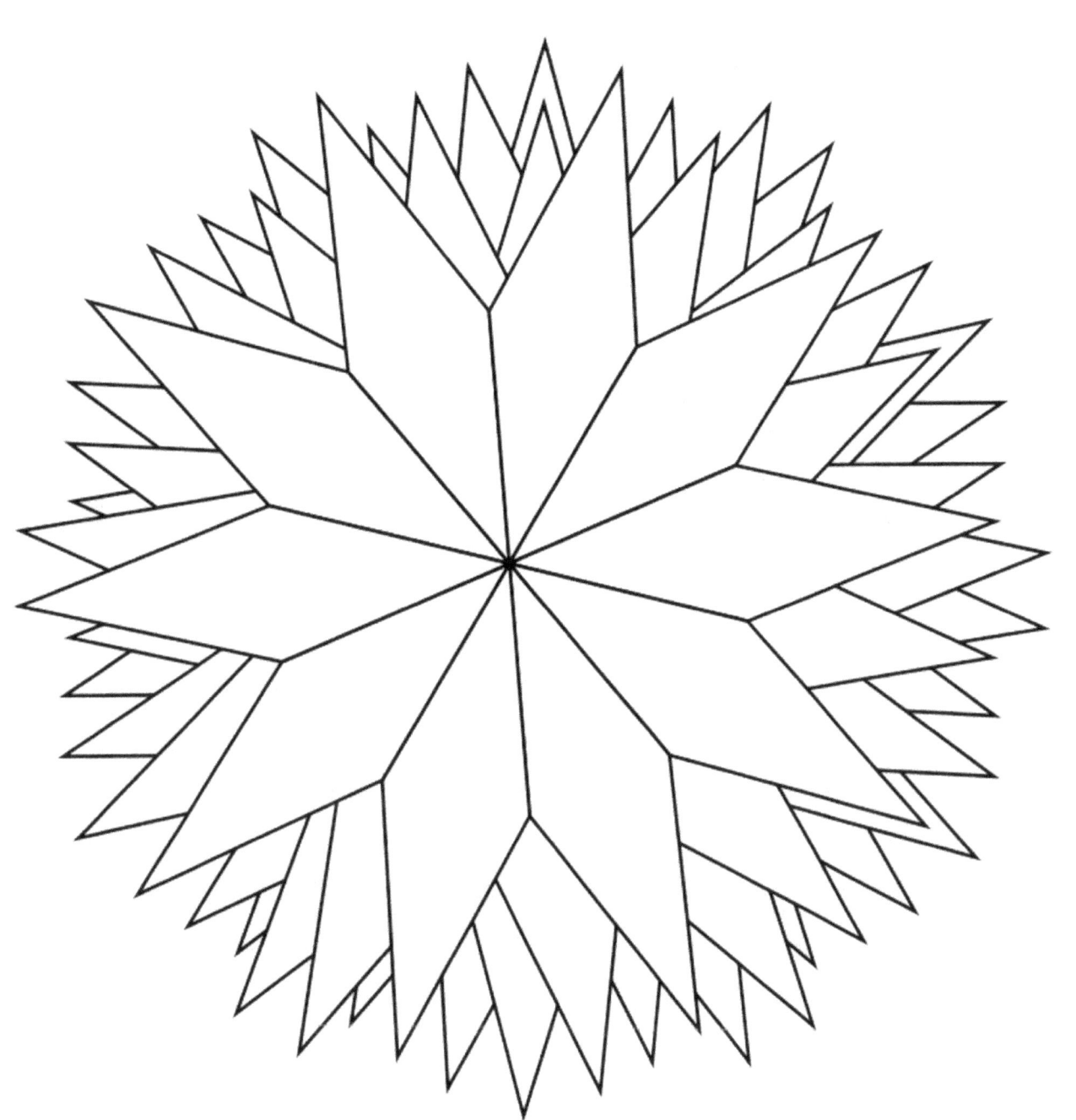

How do you feel today?

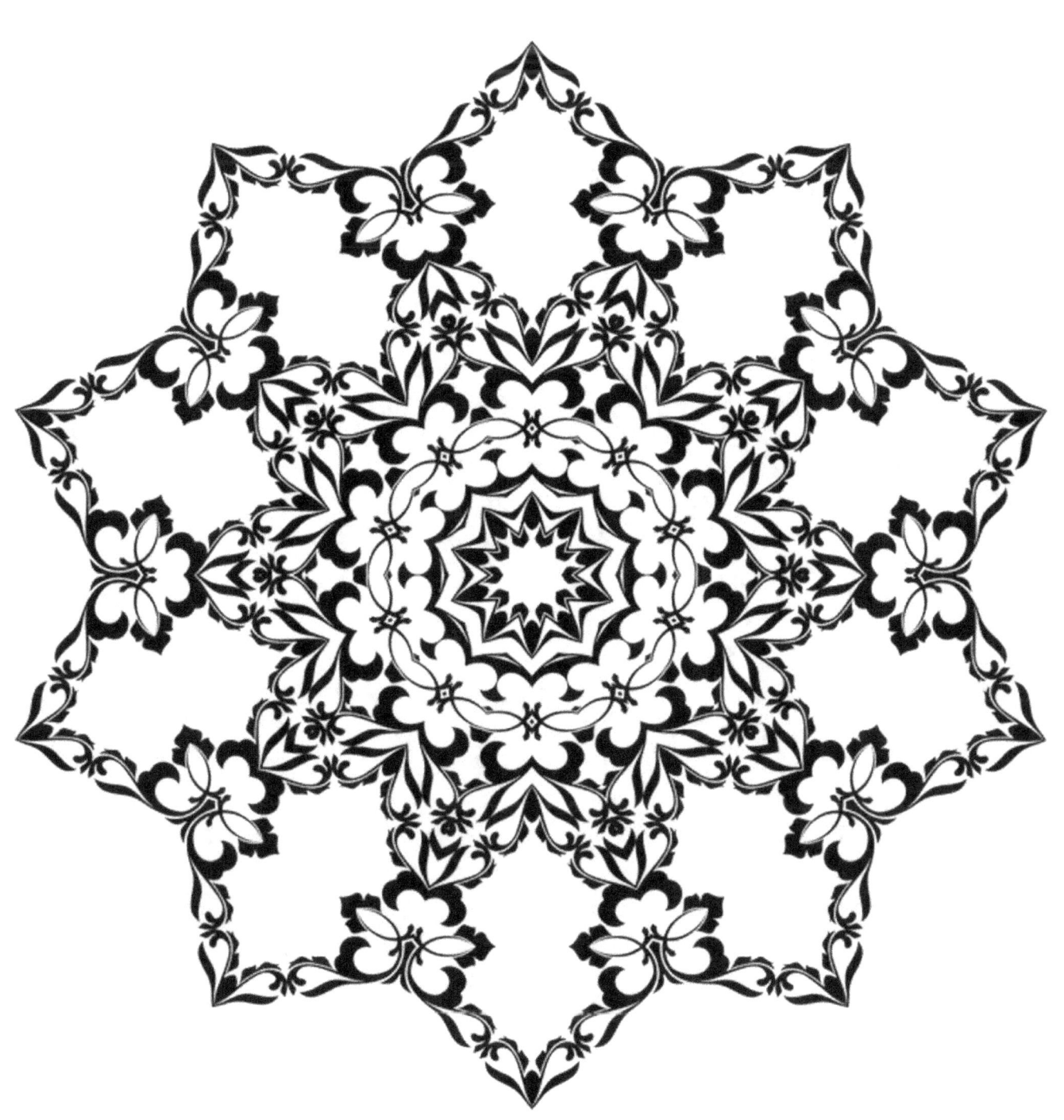

It is a beautiful day?

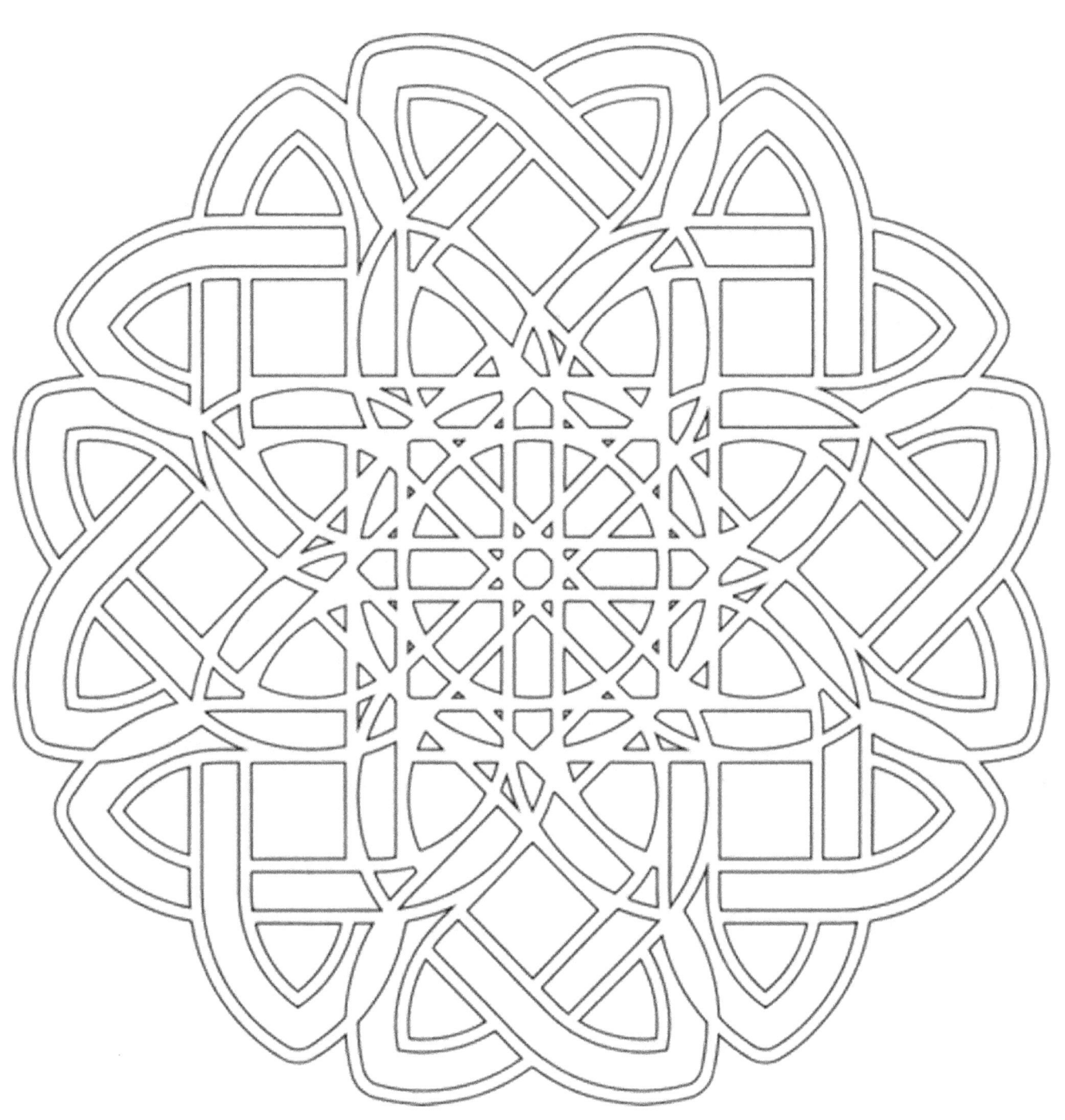

"While I am in the world, I am the light of the world."

John 9:5

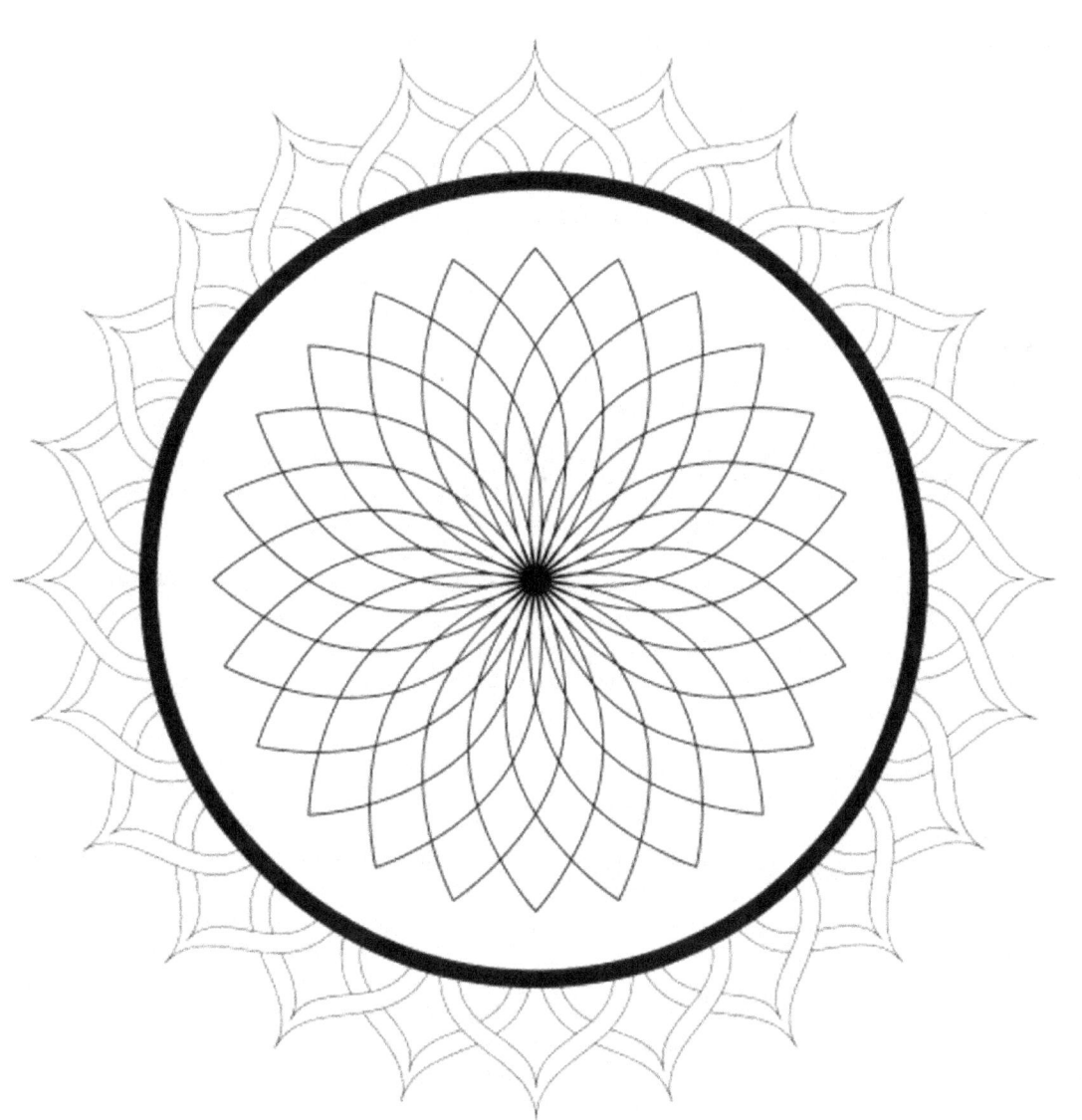

All the scriptures lead to me,

I am their author and their wisdom

From the Bhagavad Gita

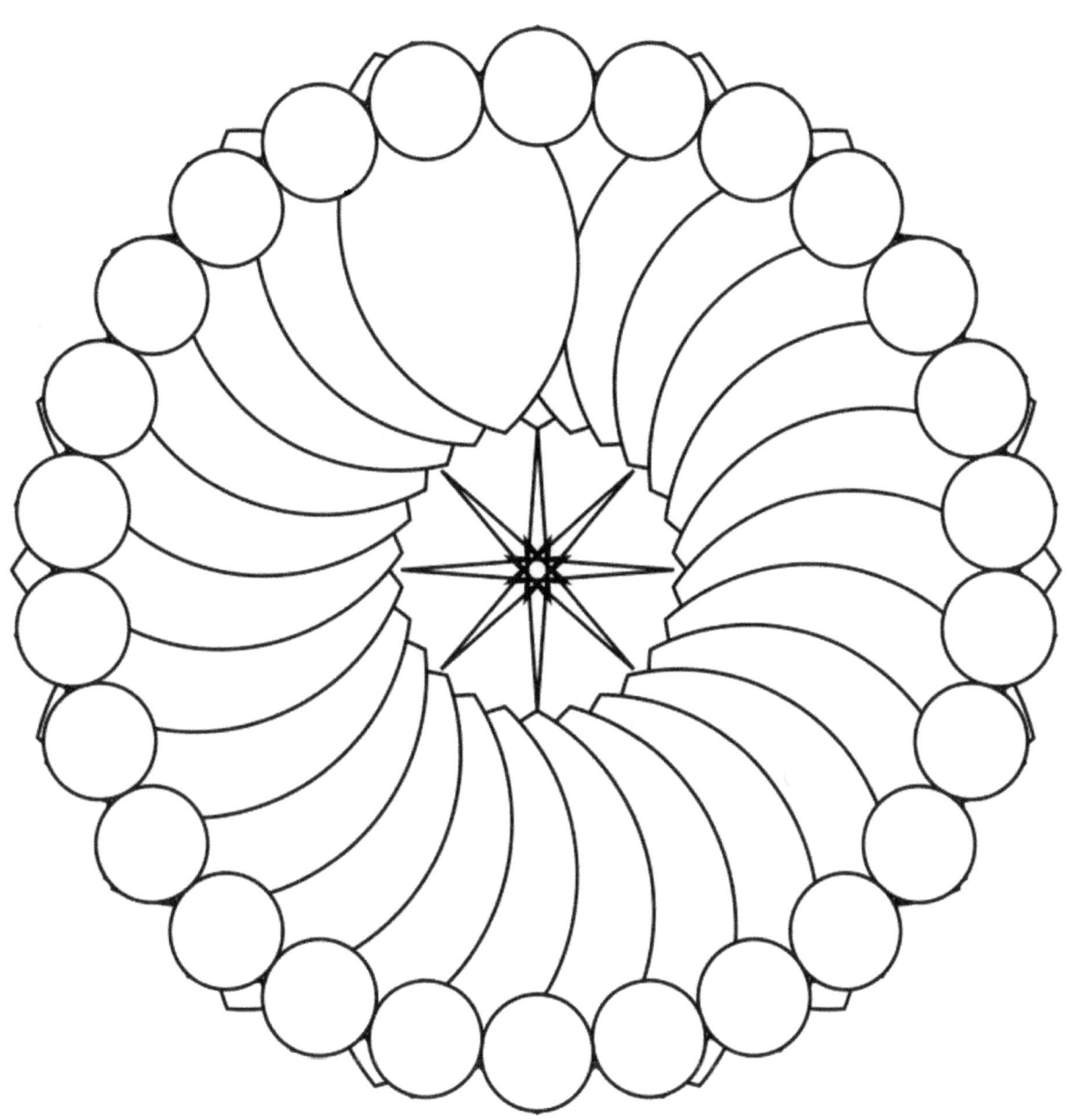

I am grateful today.

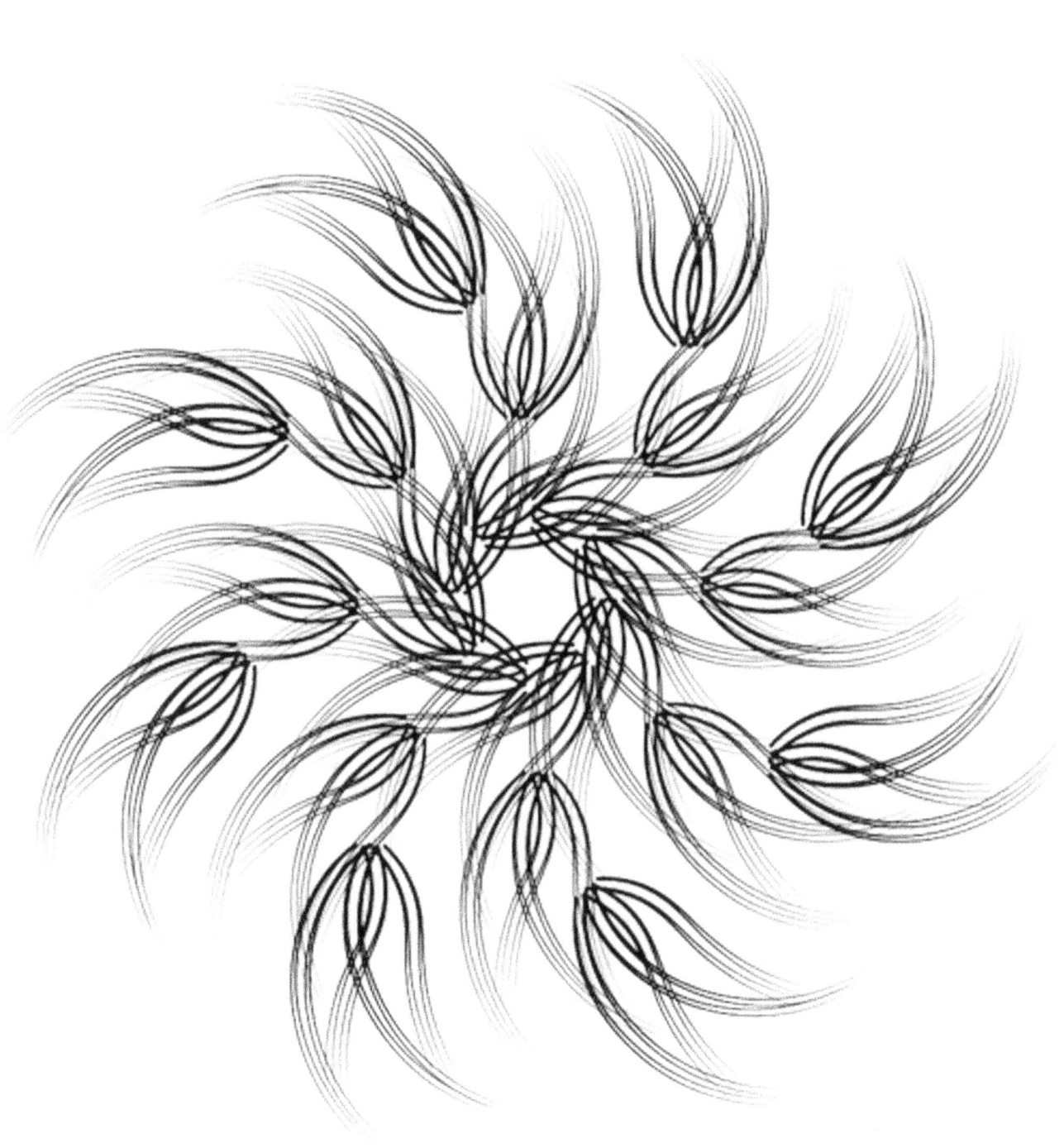

I am blessed.

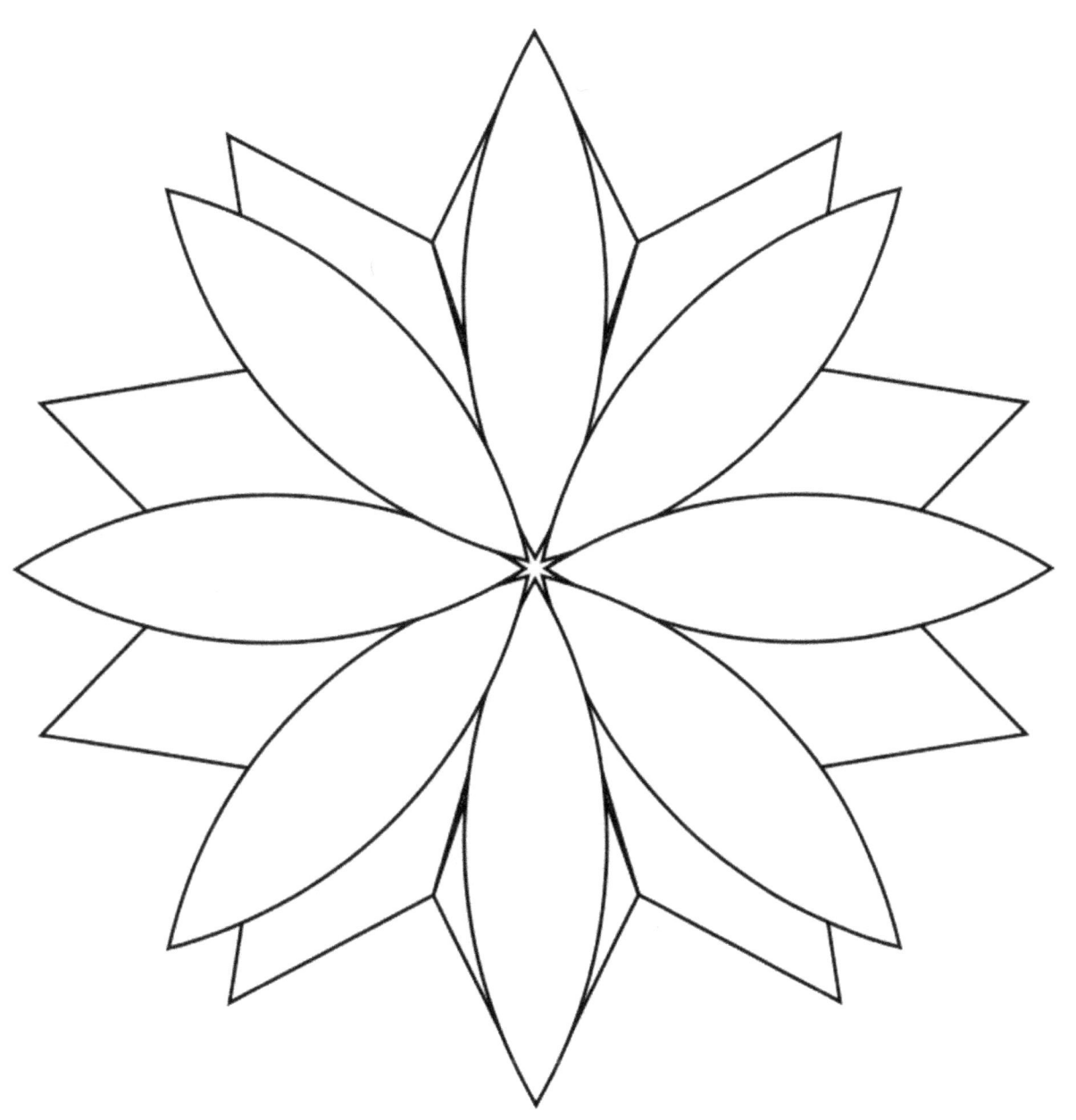

I love myself.

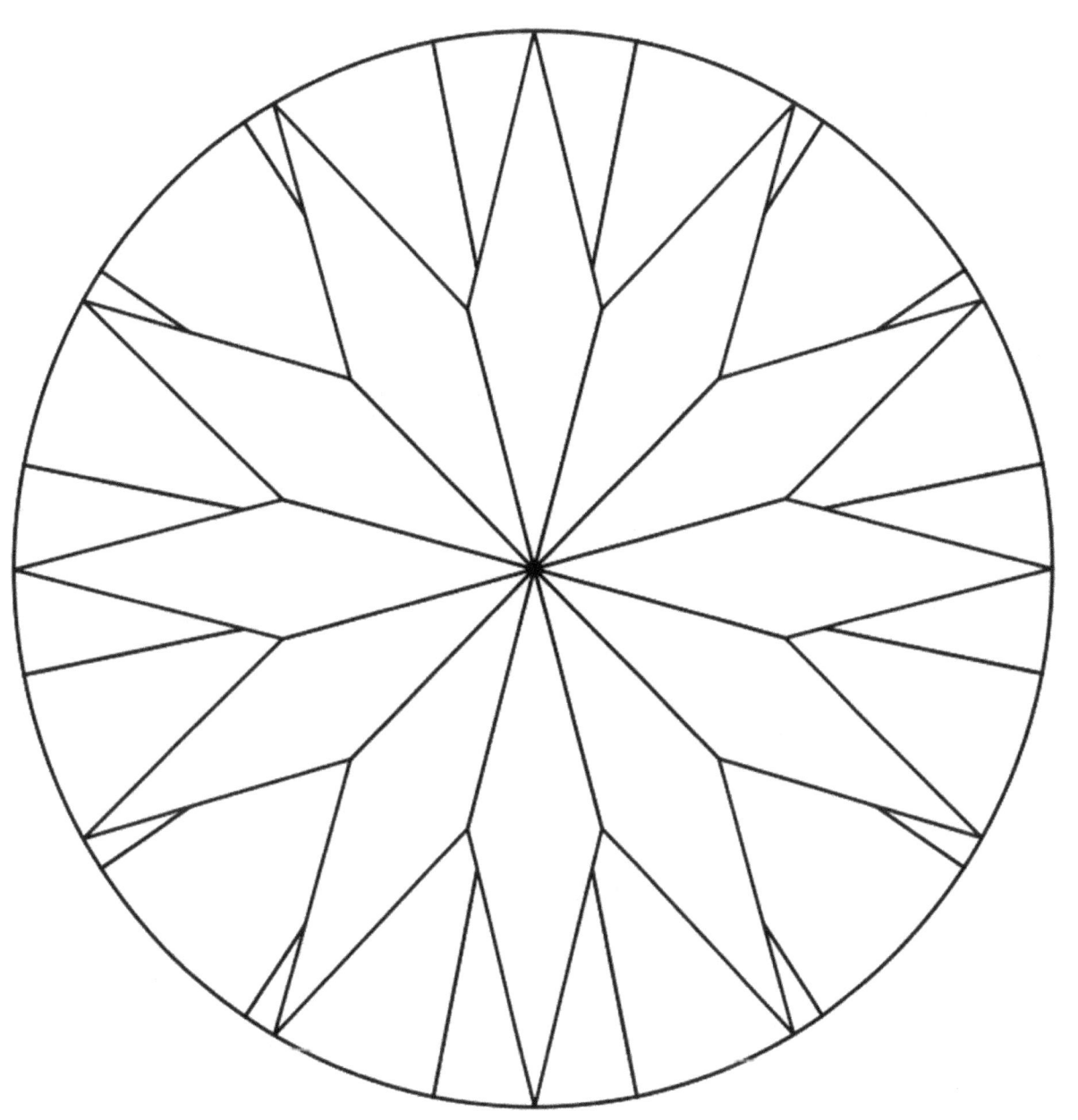

Seek peace

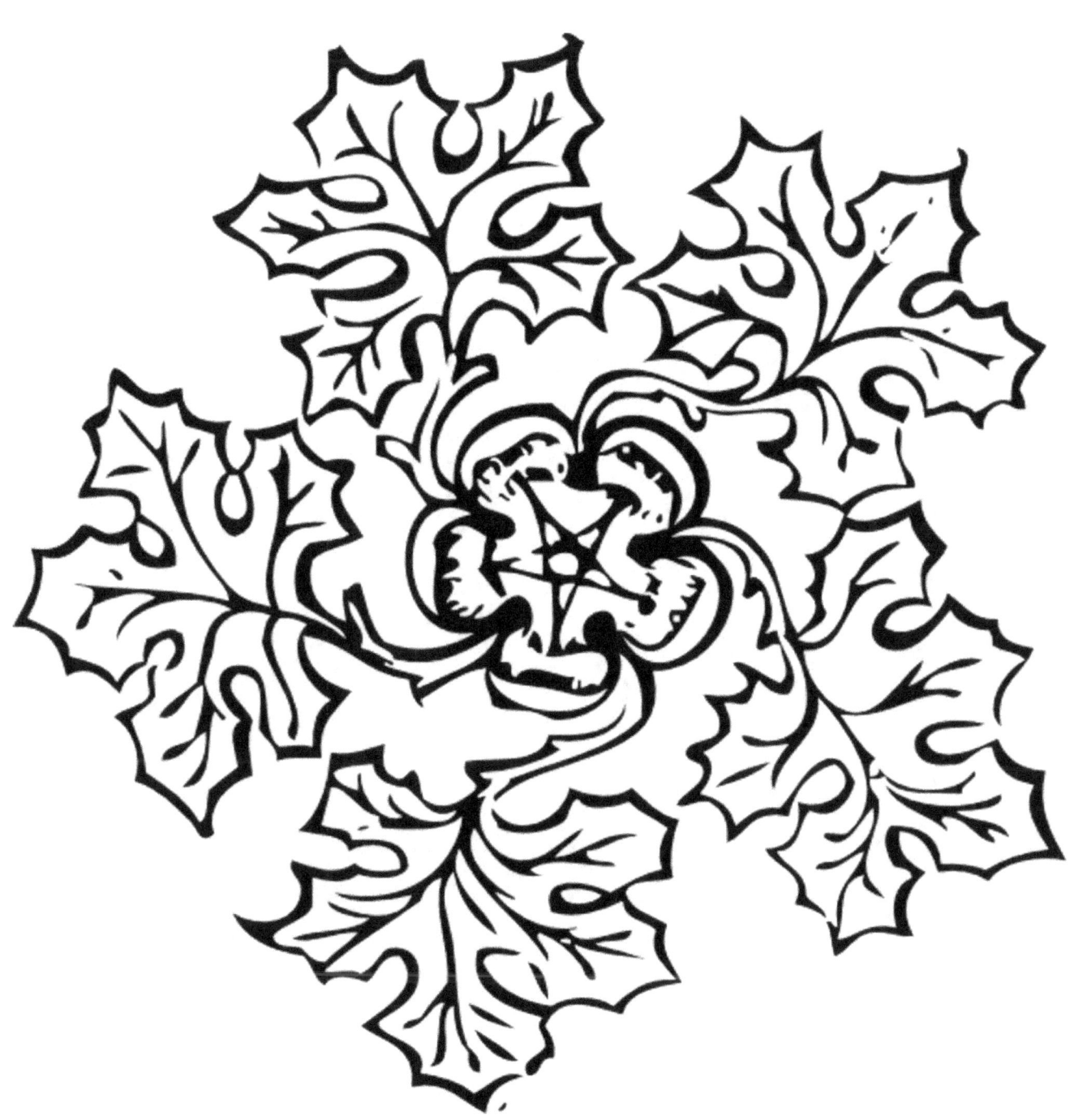

Friends are forever

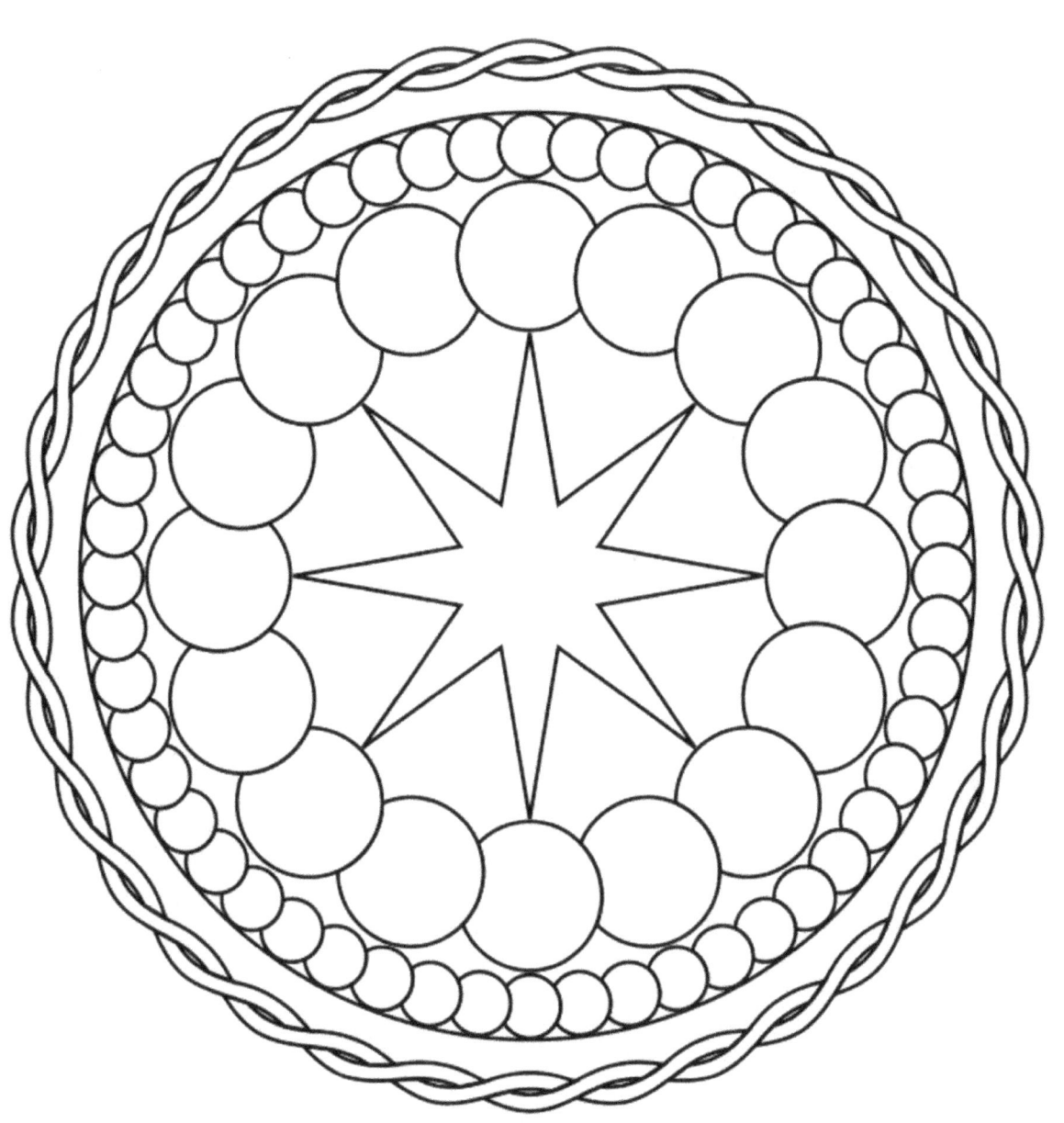

Forgive someone today

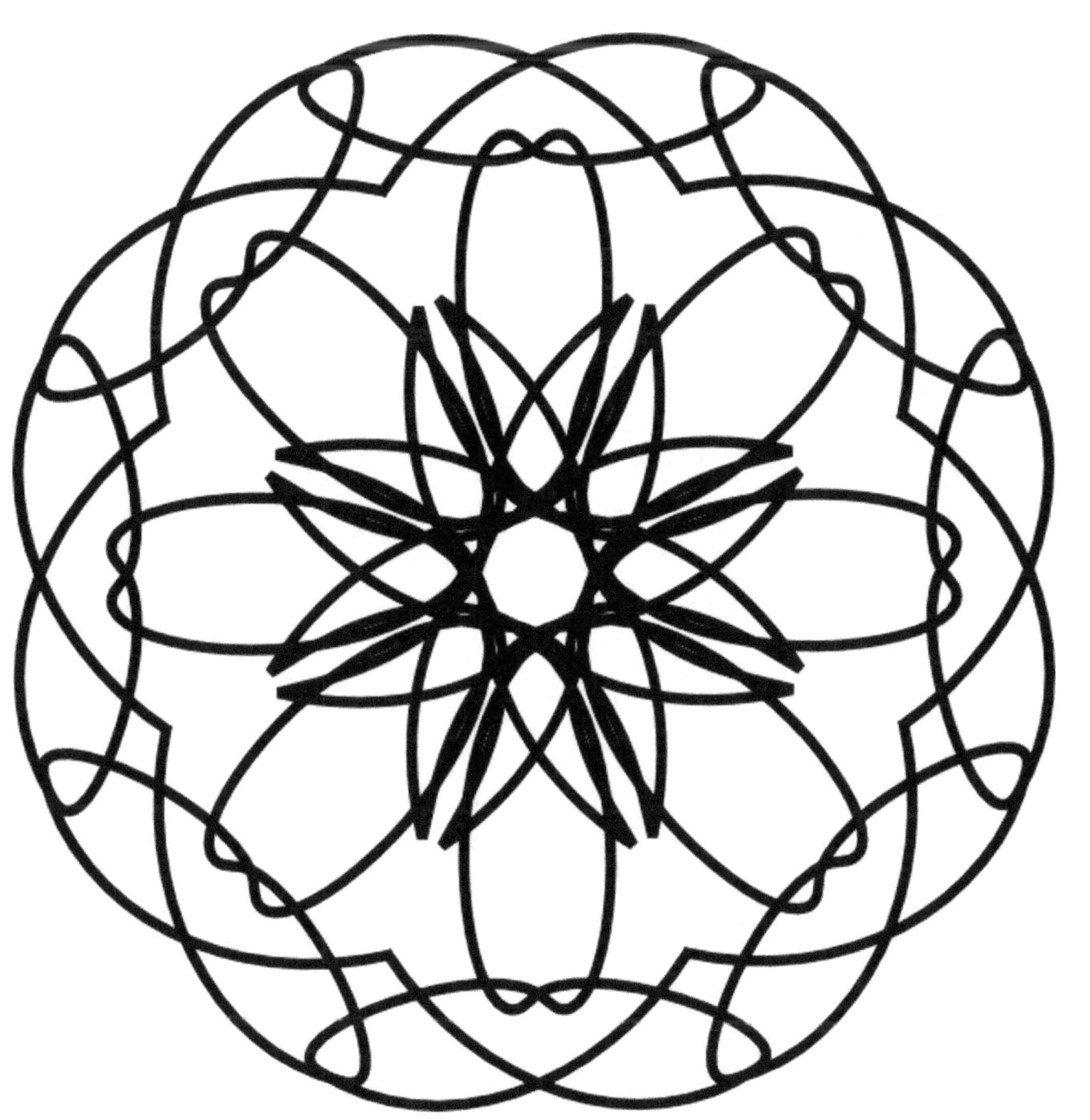

Don't let anything or anyone

destroy your peace

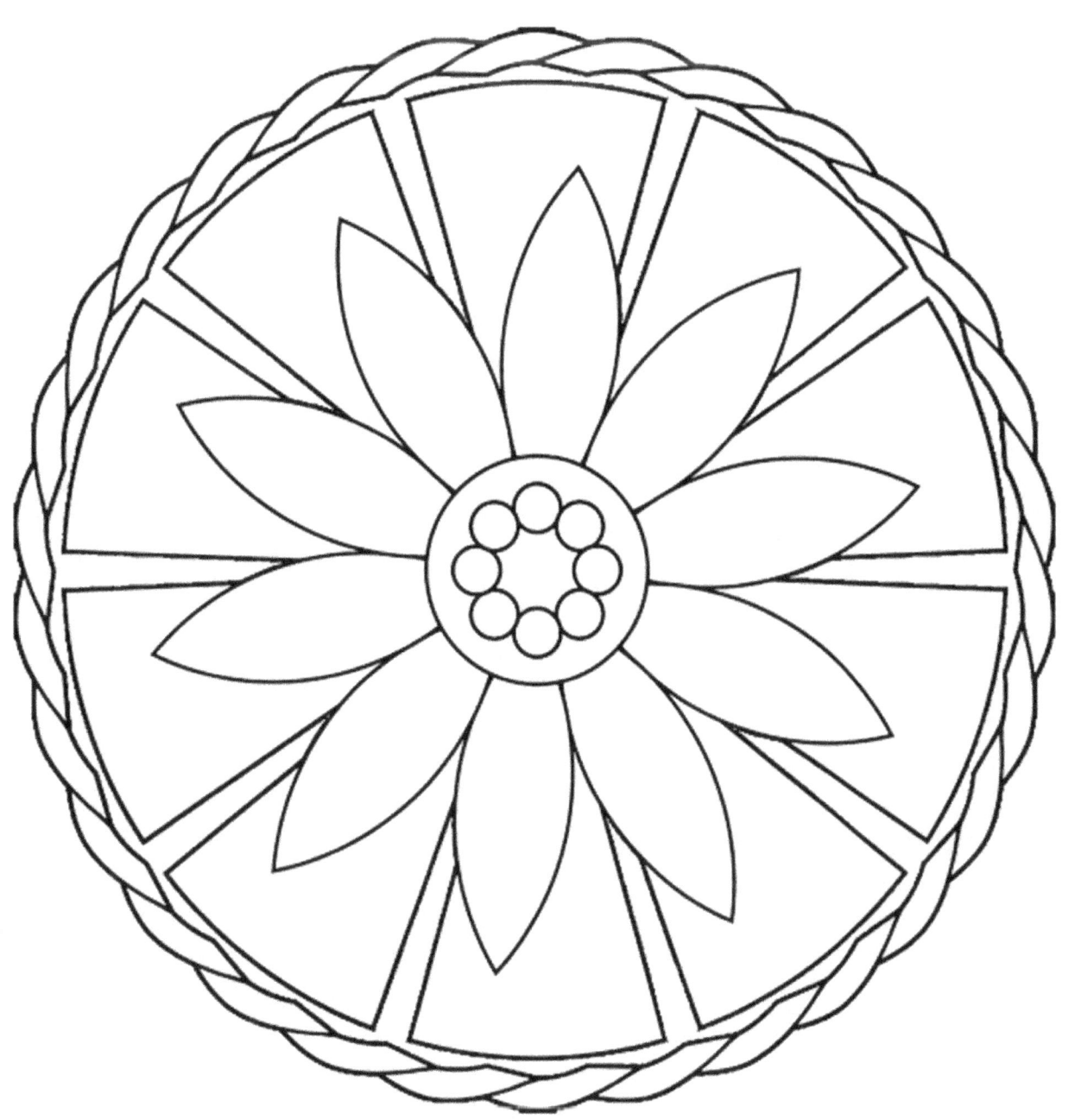

Did you hug someone today?

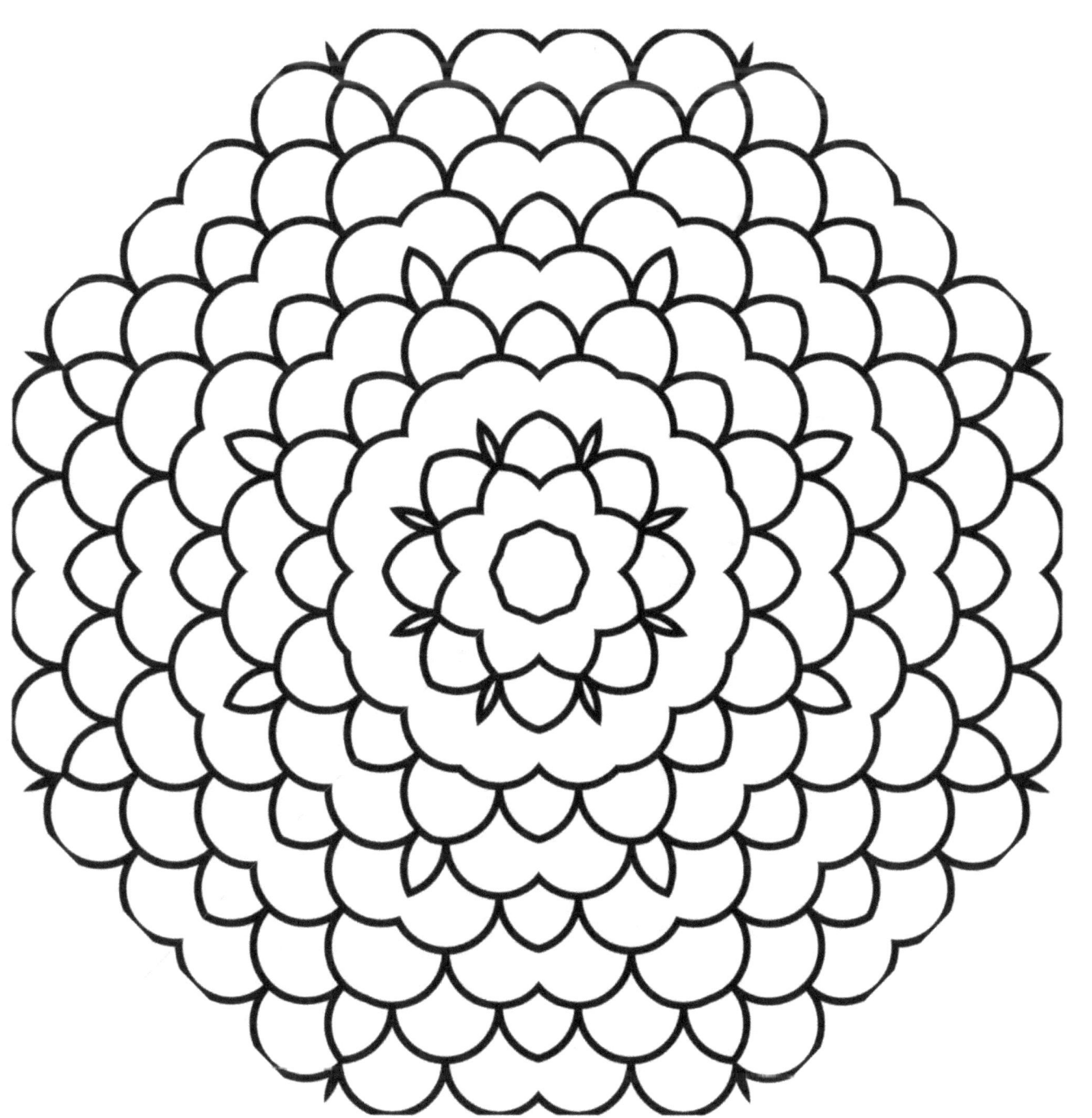

Let peace flow within you

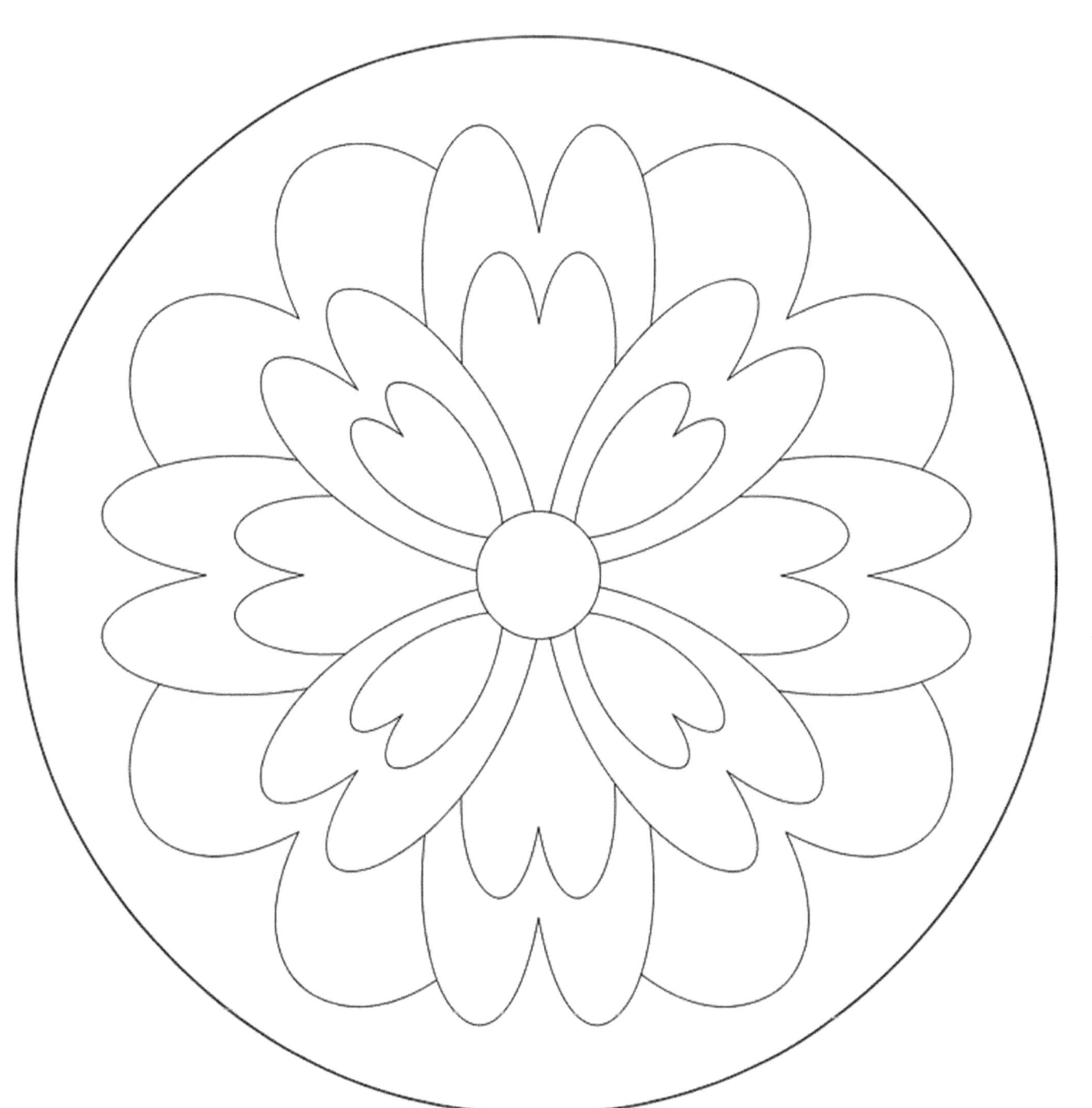

I am a conqueror

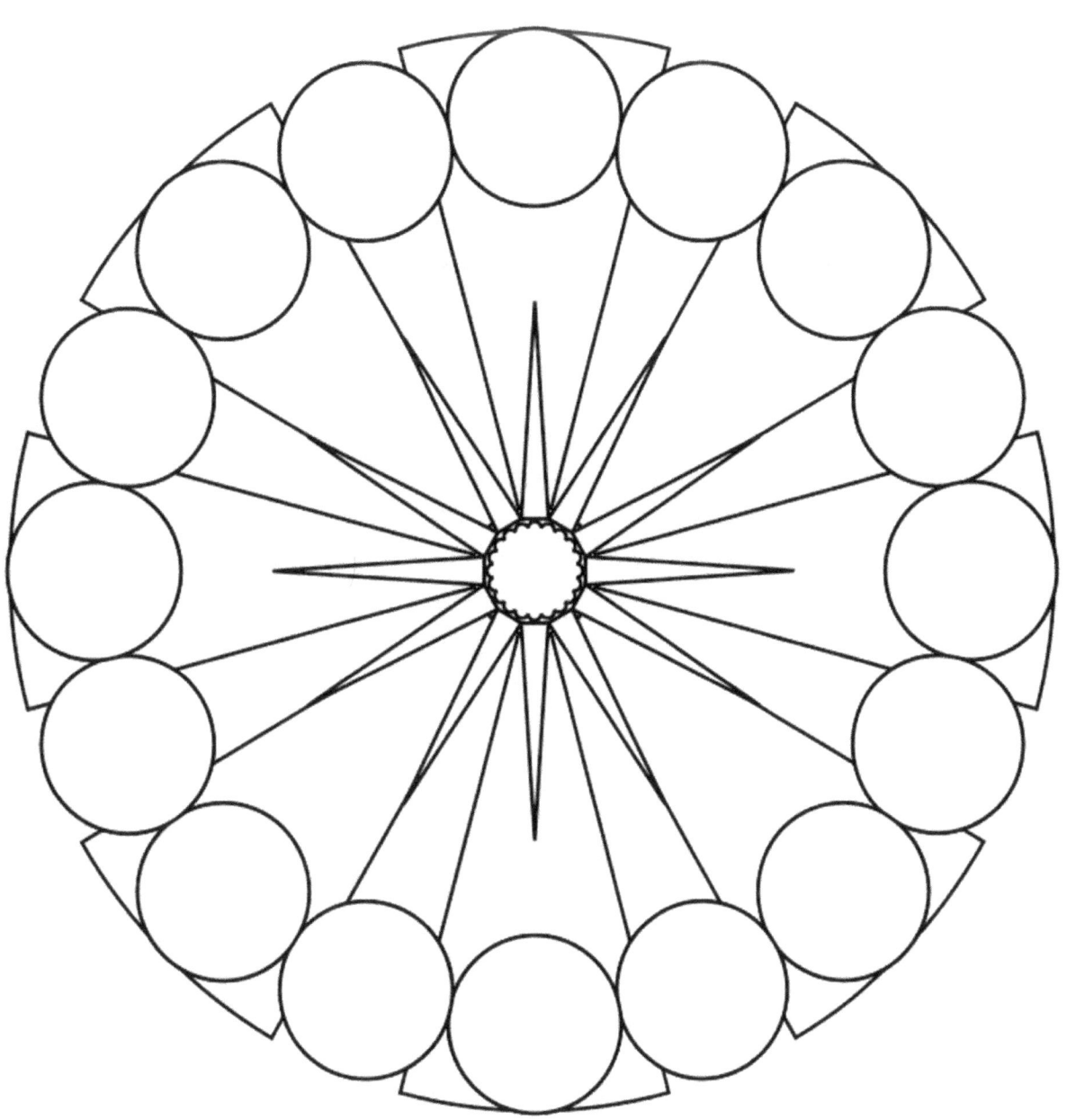

Did you give someone a smile today

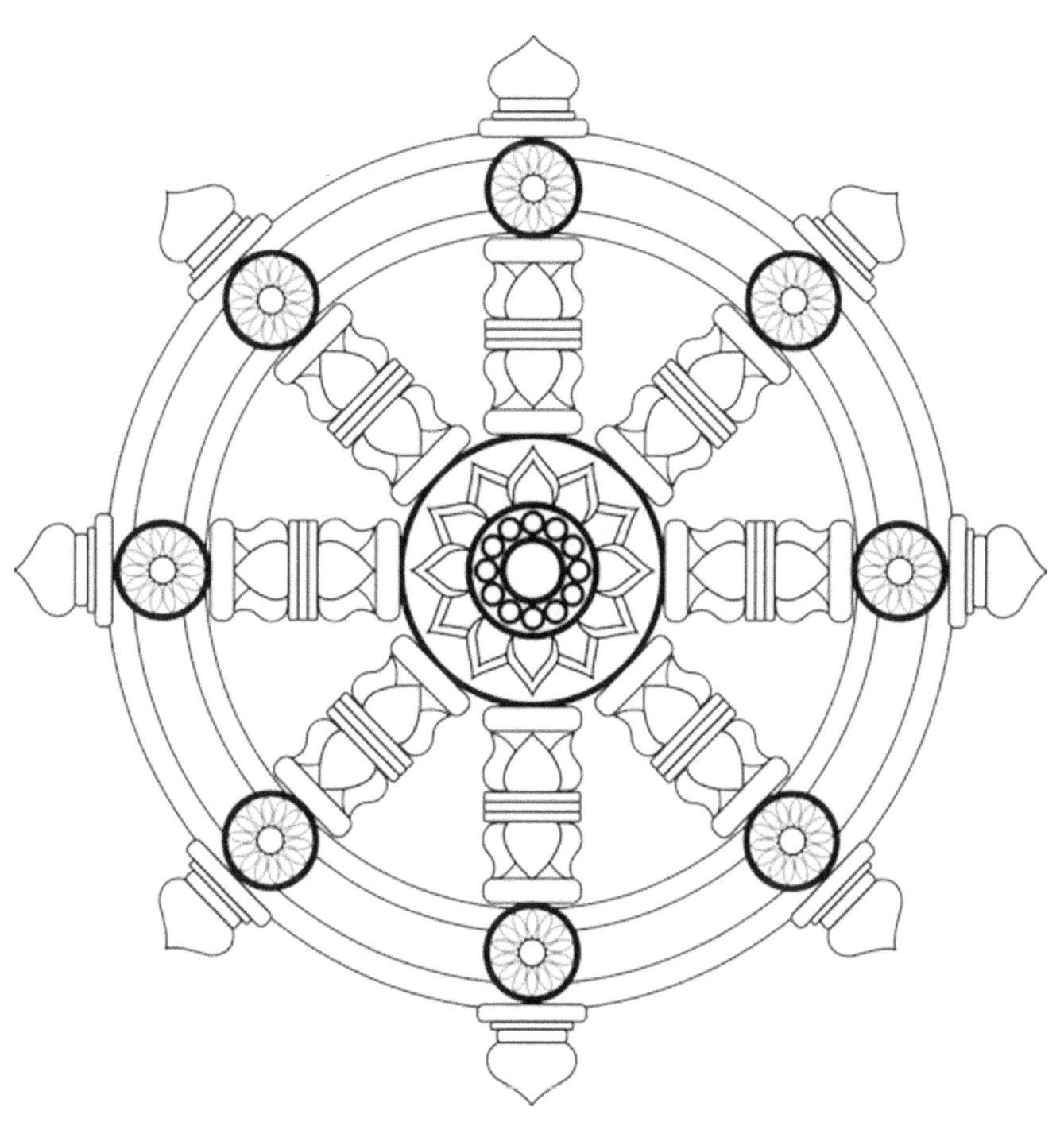

Judge not, that ye be not judged.

St. Mathew 7:1

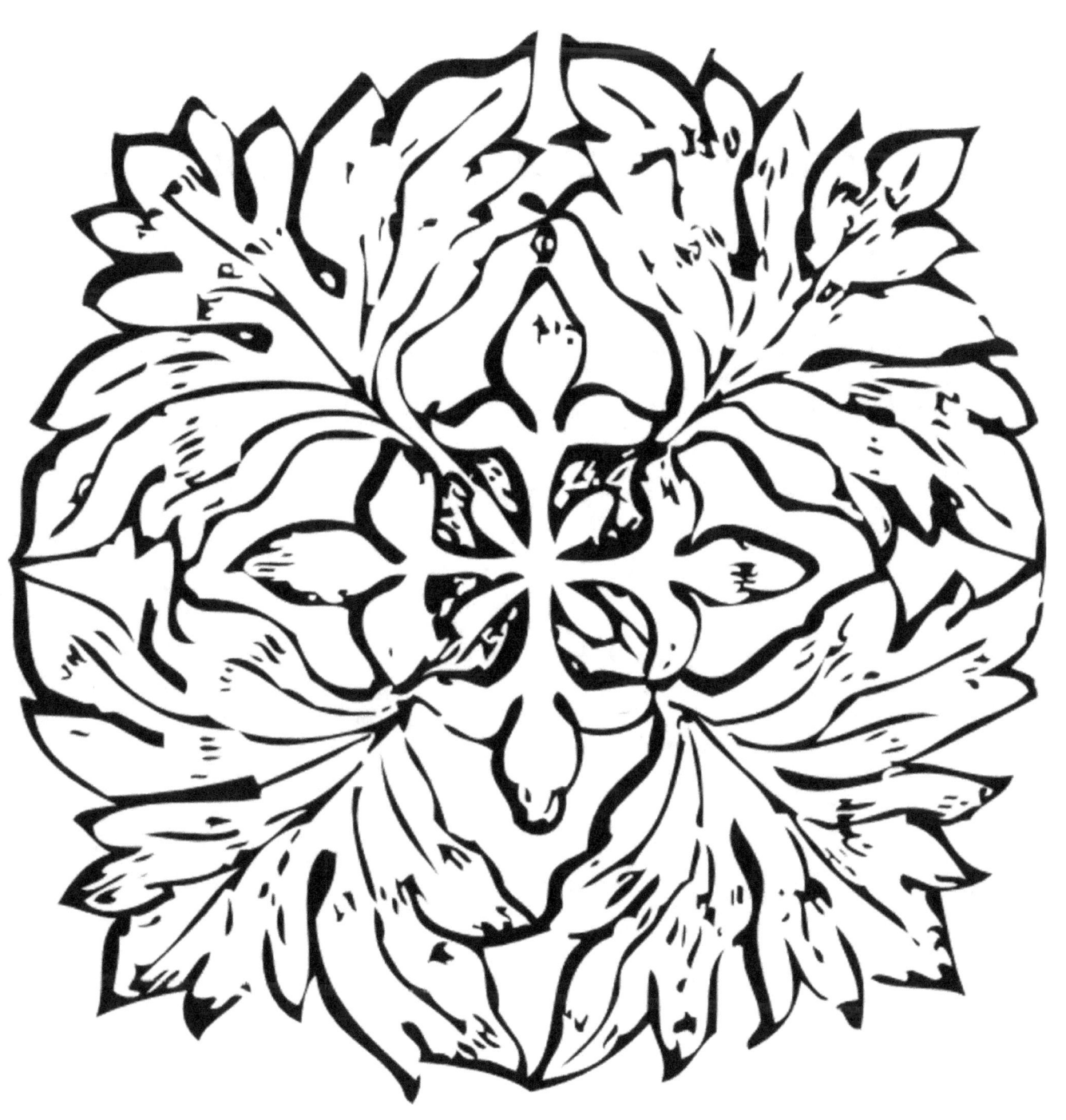

For where your treasure is, there your heart will be also.

St. Mathew 6:21

The Kingdom of God is with you.

St. Luke 16:21

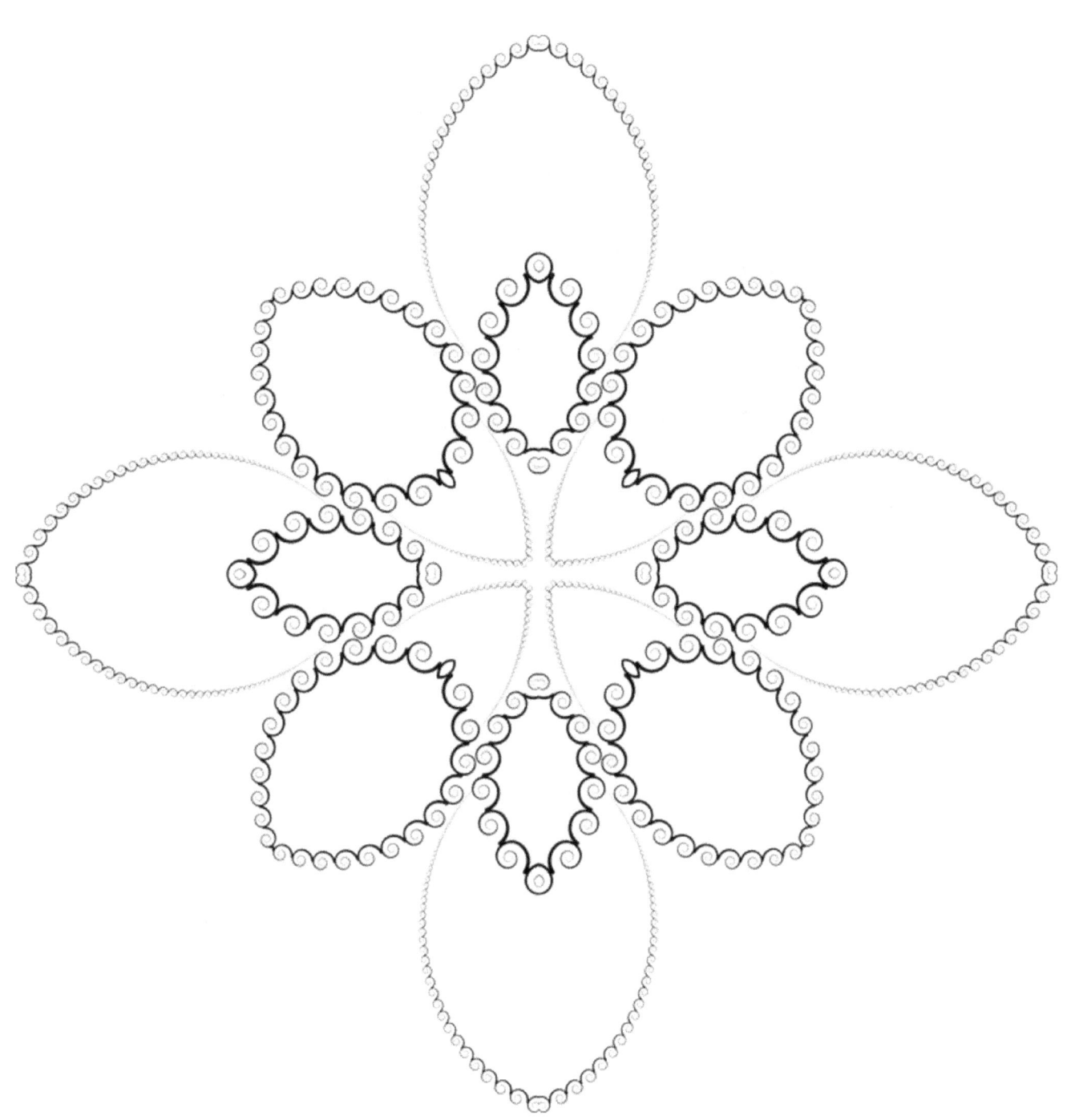

Happiness is your nature,

It is not wrong to desire it.

What is wrong is seeking it outside

When it is inside

Ramana Maharshi

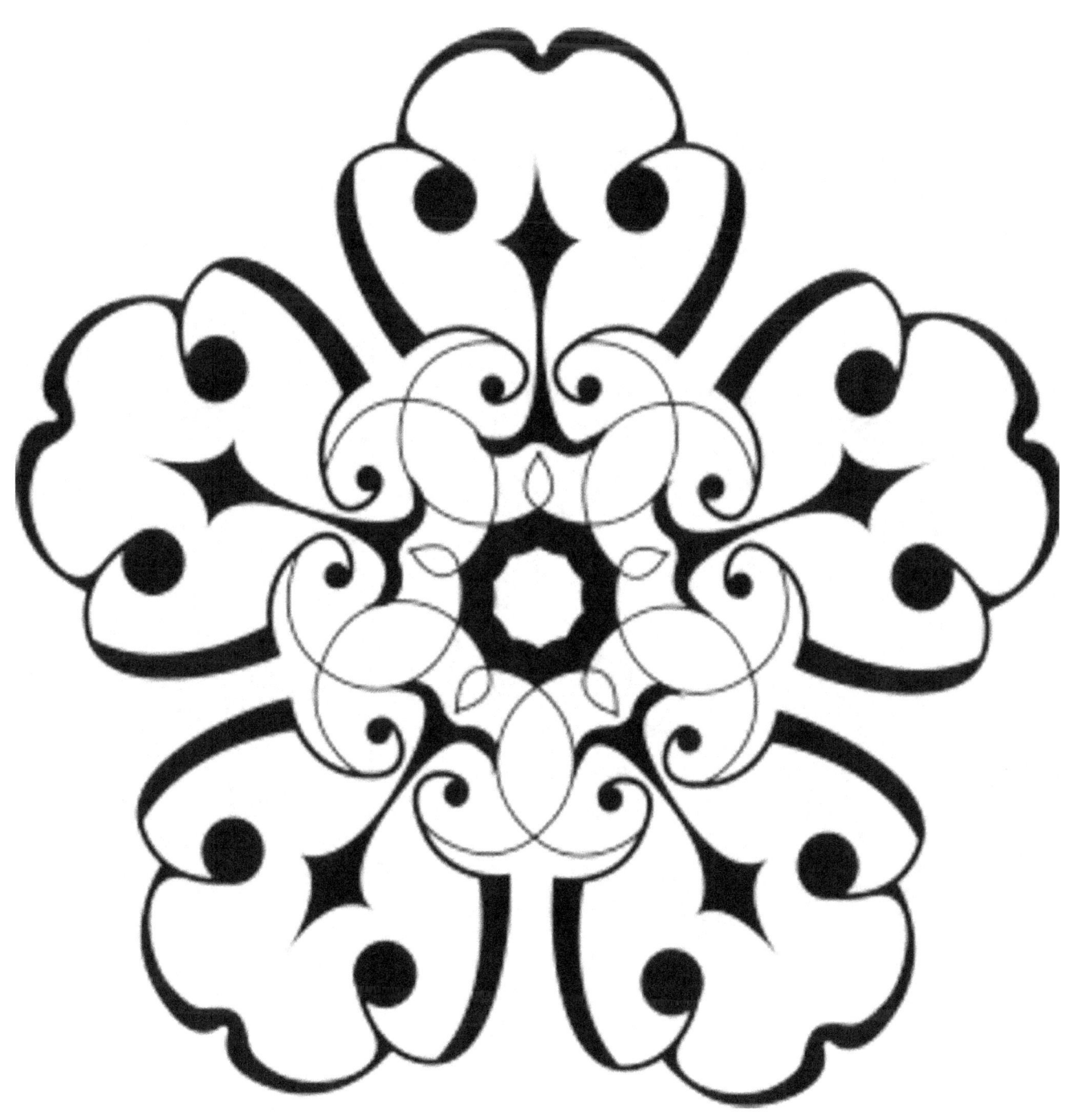

"For you are my lamp O Lord, and the Lord illumines my darkness"

2 Samuel 22:29

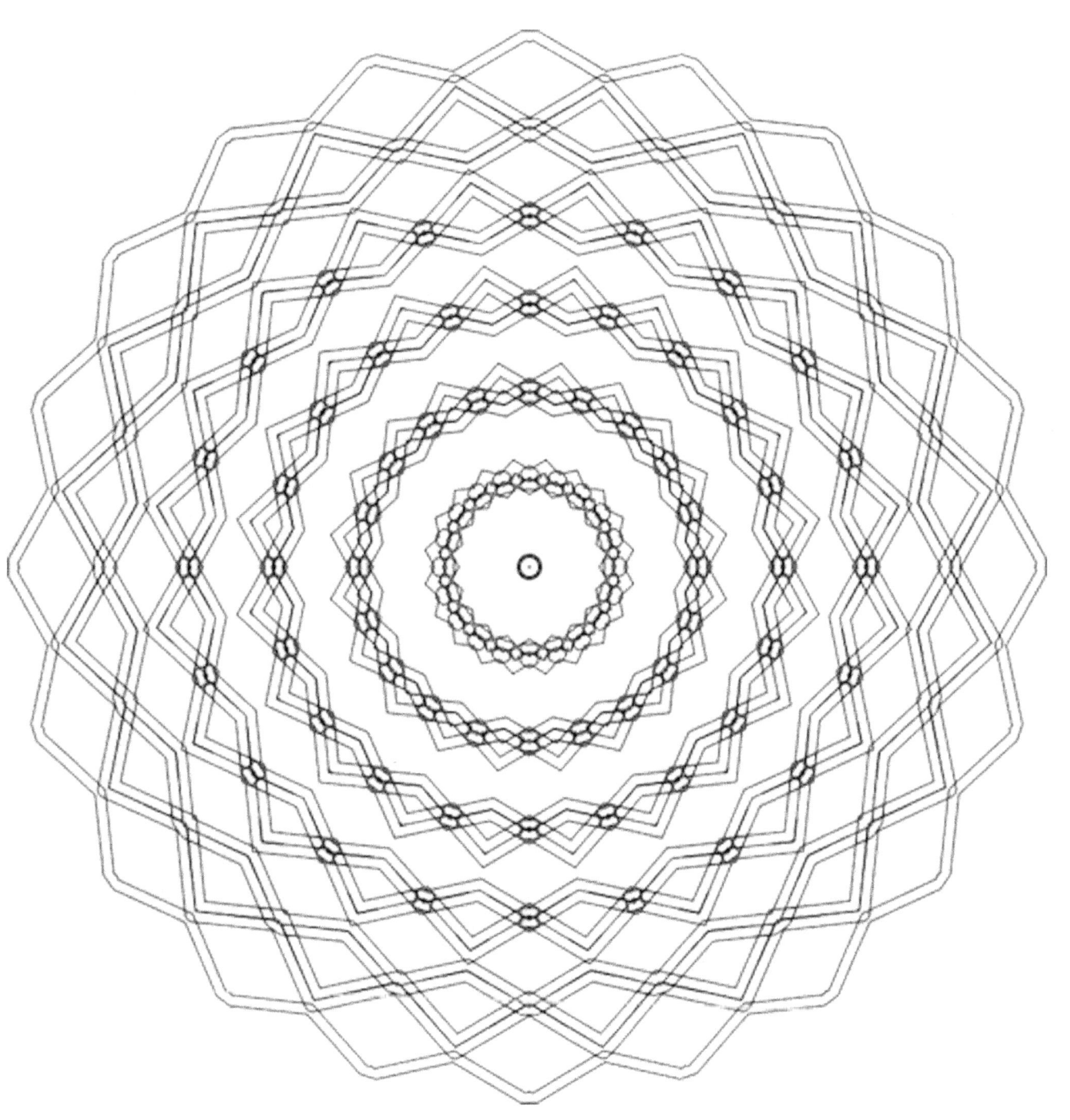

Man is made by his belief

As he believes, so he is.

From the Bhagavad Gita

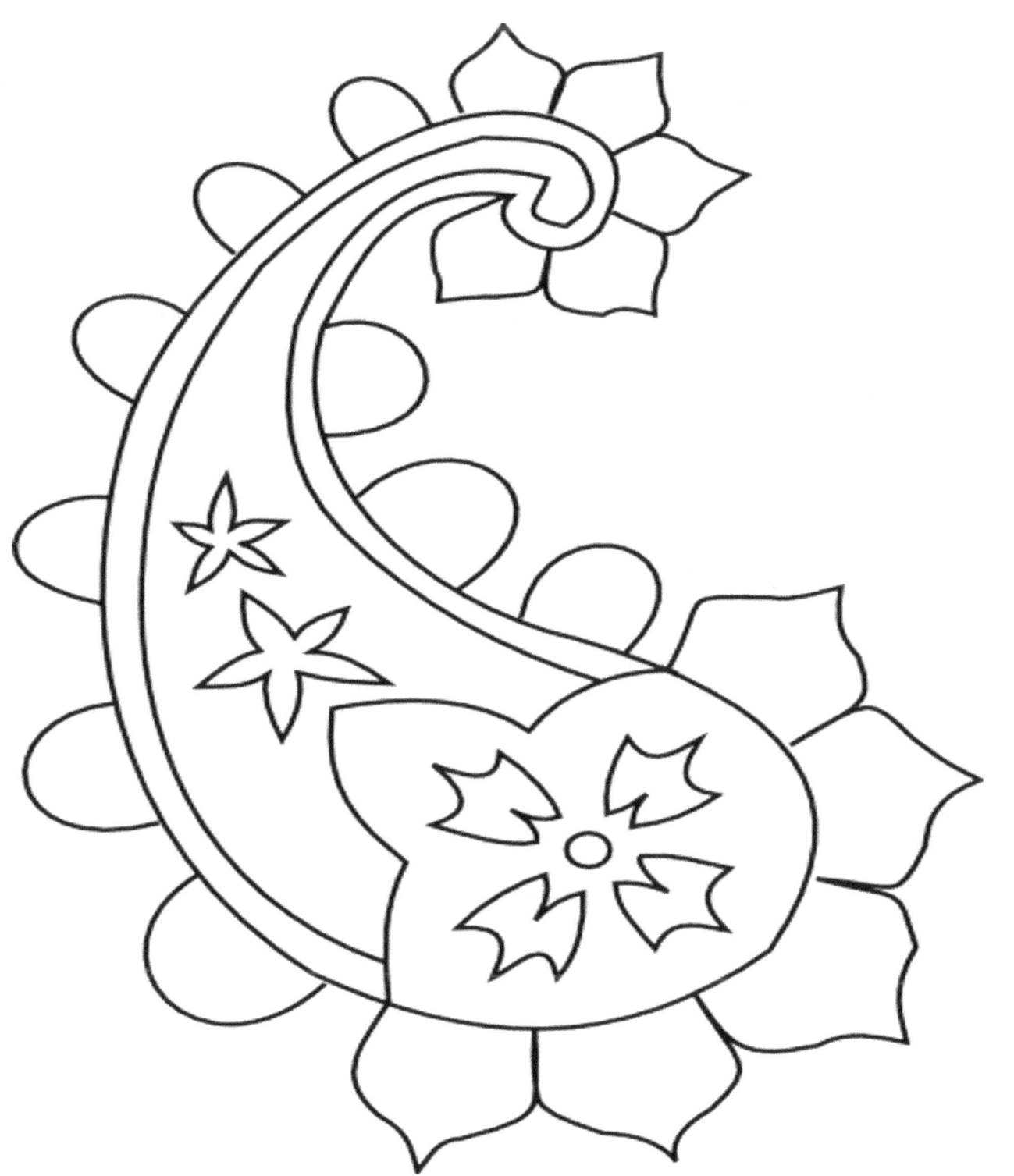

Out of clutter find simplicity,

From discord, find harmony

In the middle of difficulty lies opprtunity

Albert Einstein

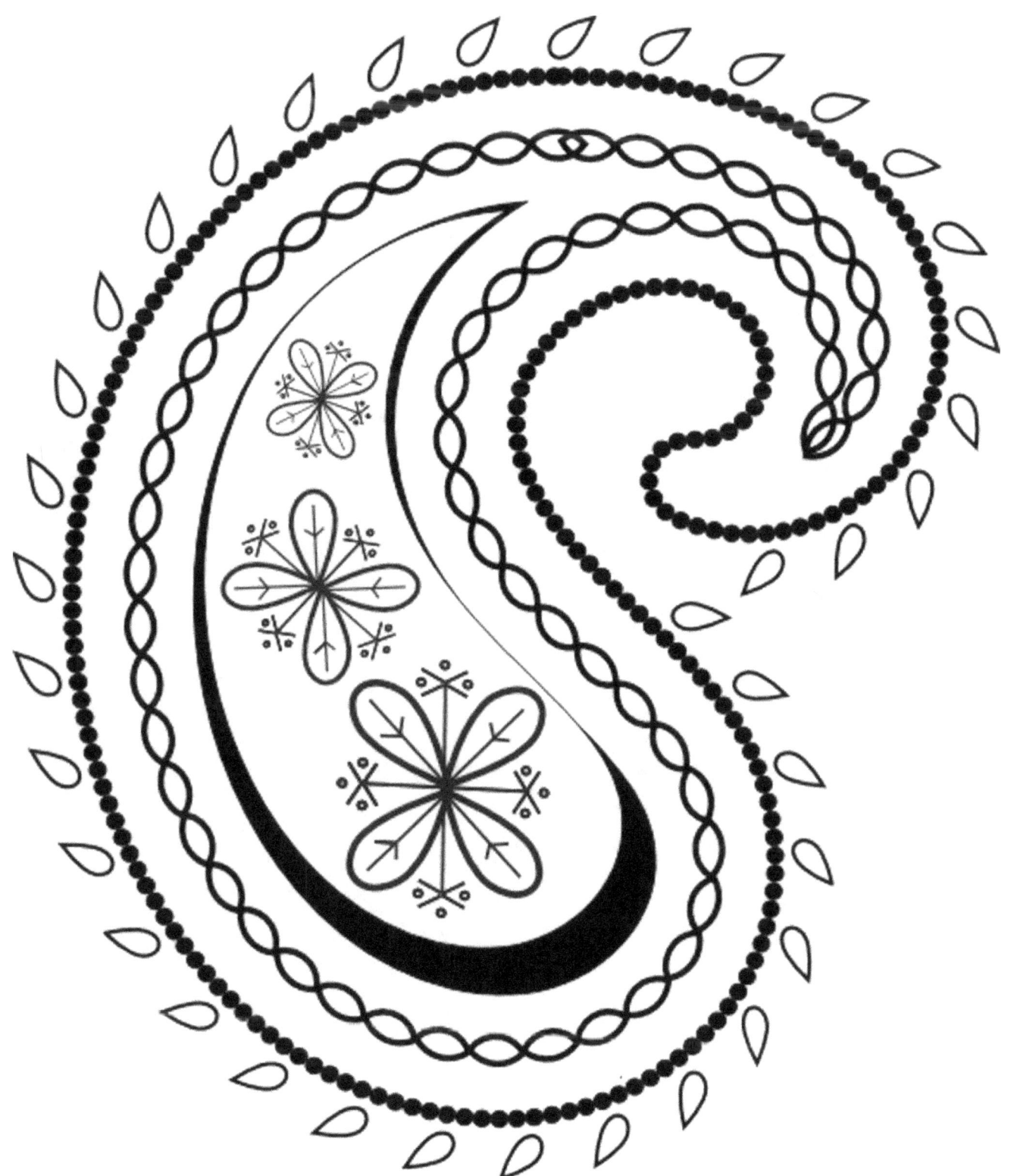

Did you laugh today?

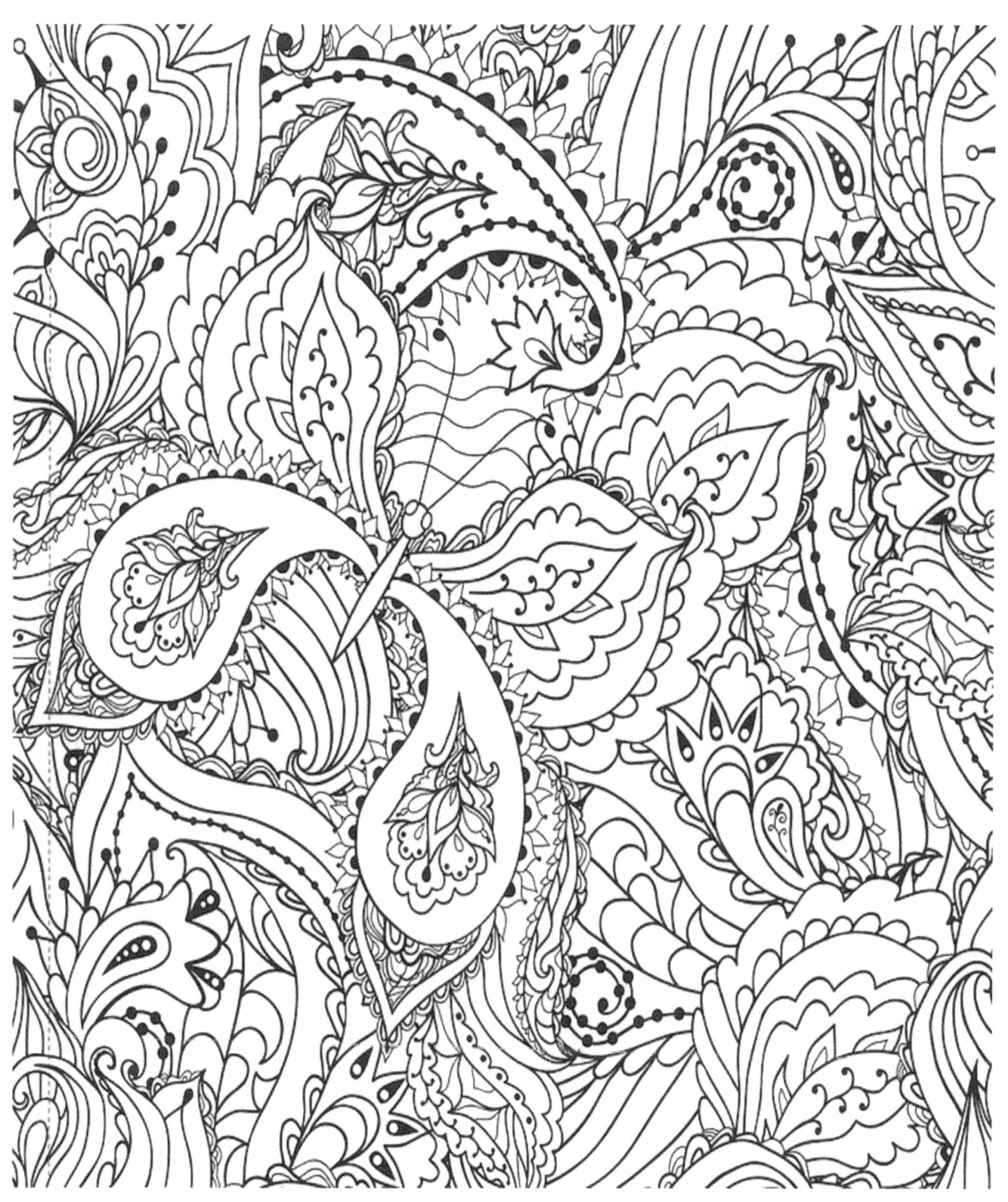

The secret os human freedom is

to act well.

Without attachments to the results

From the Bhagvat Gita

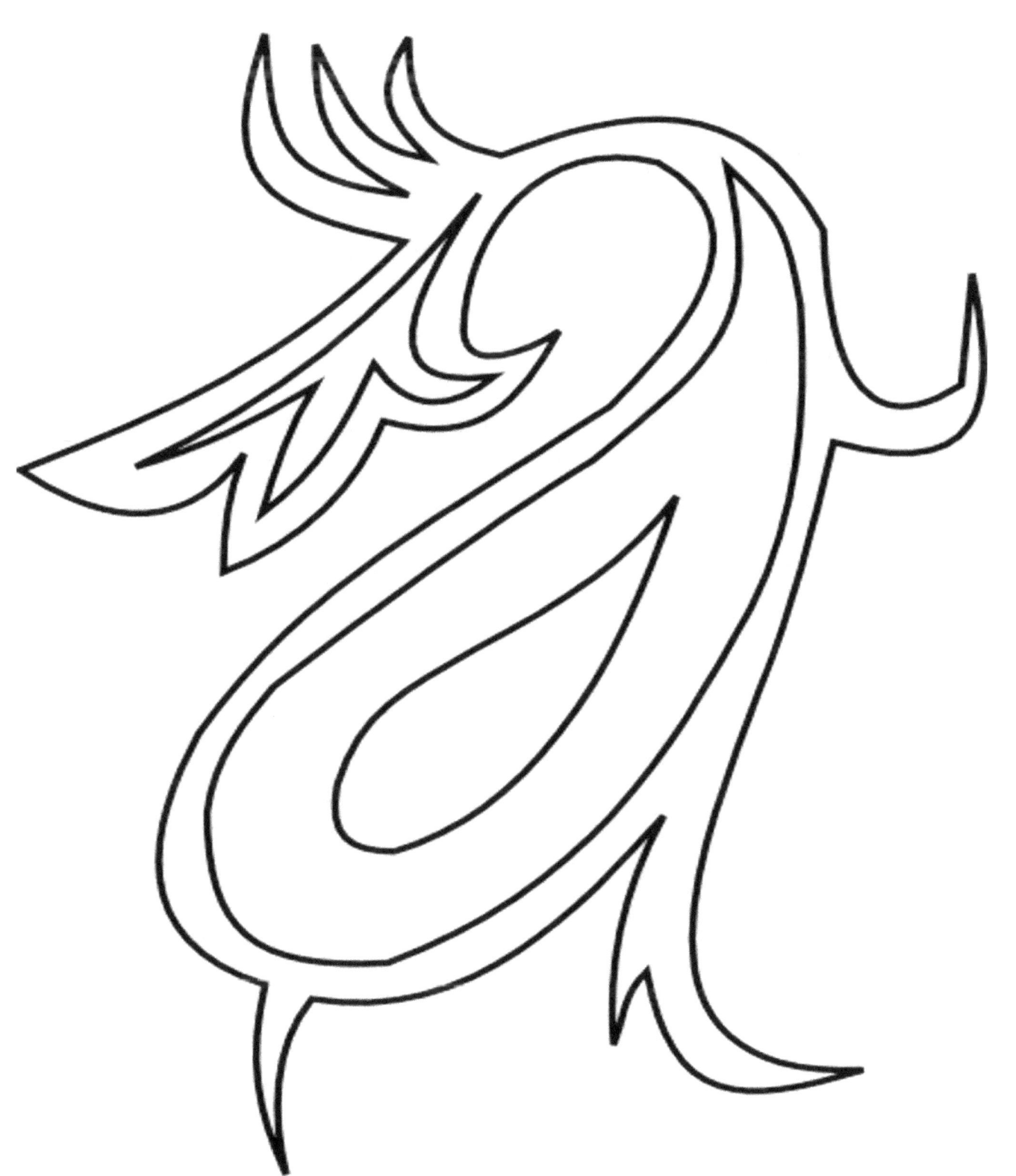

Your own Self-Realization   is the

Greatest service you can render the world

Ramana Maharshi

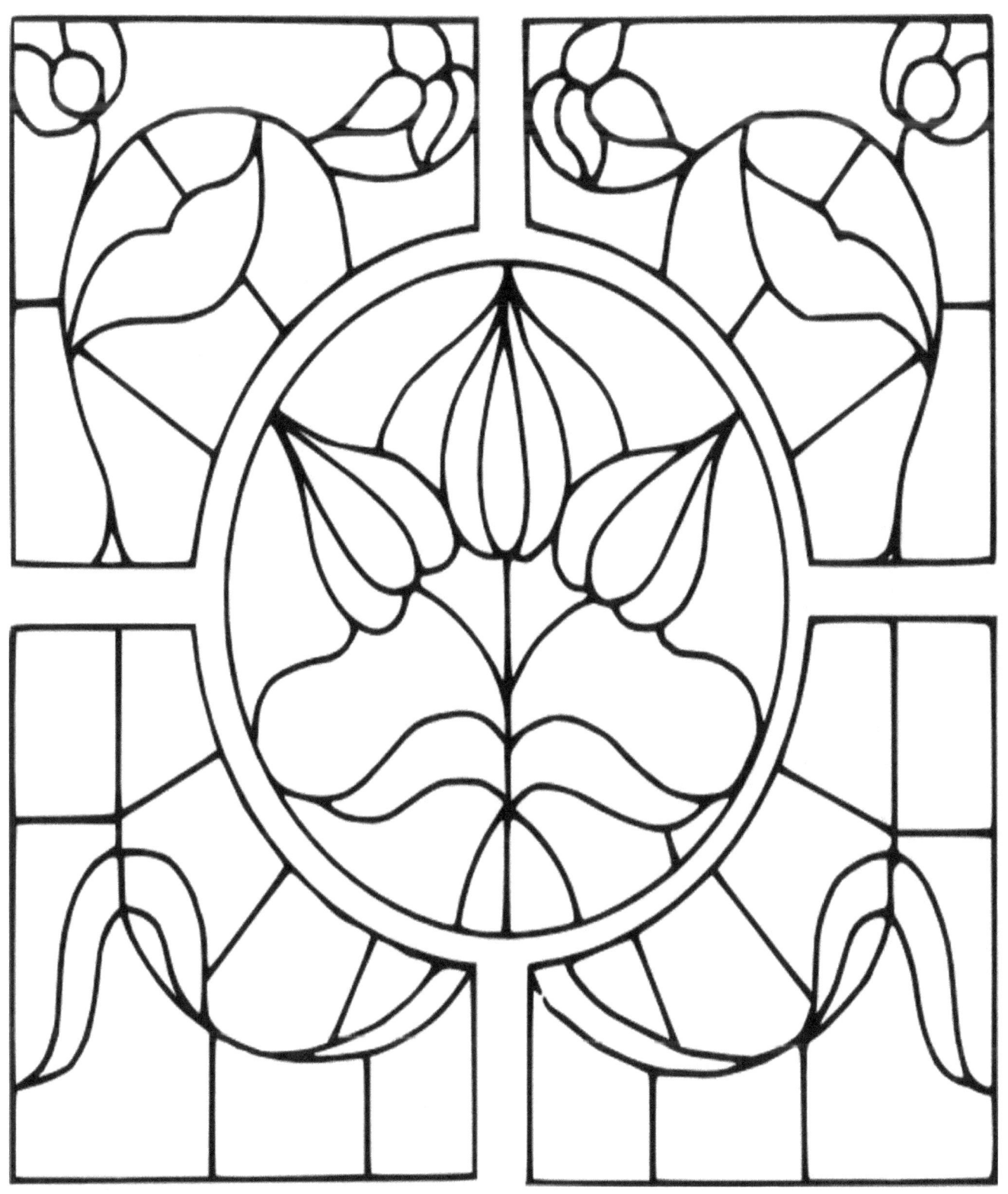

Never, never , never, give up

Winston Churchill

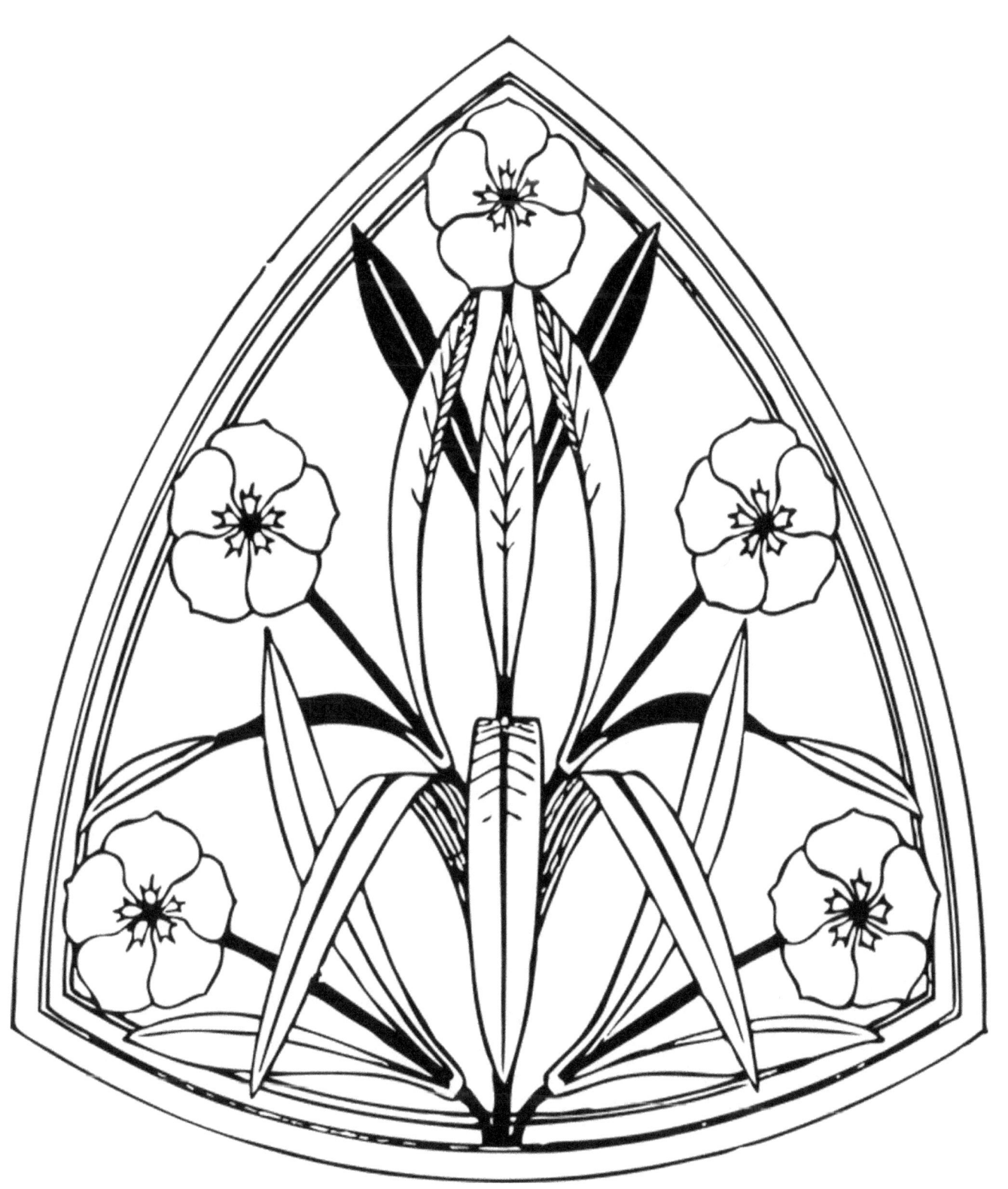

Laugh like you never laughed before

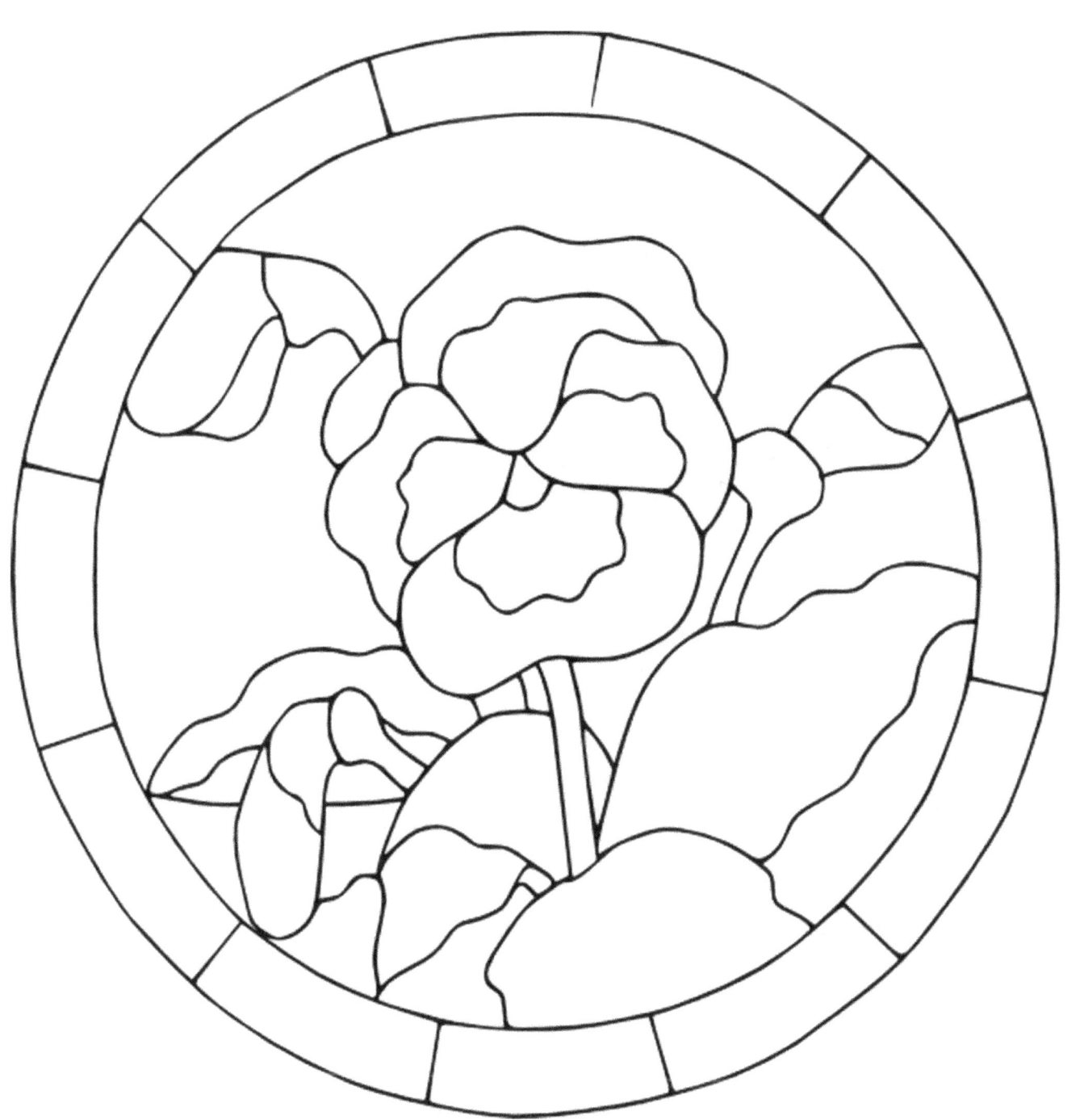

The secret of the human freedom is to act well,

Without attachment to the results

From the Bhagavad Gita

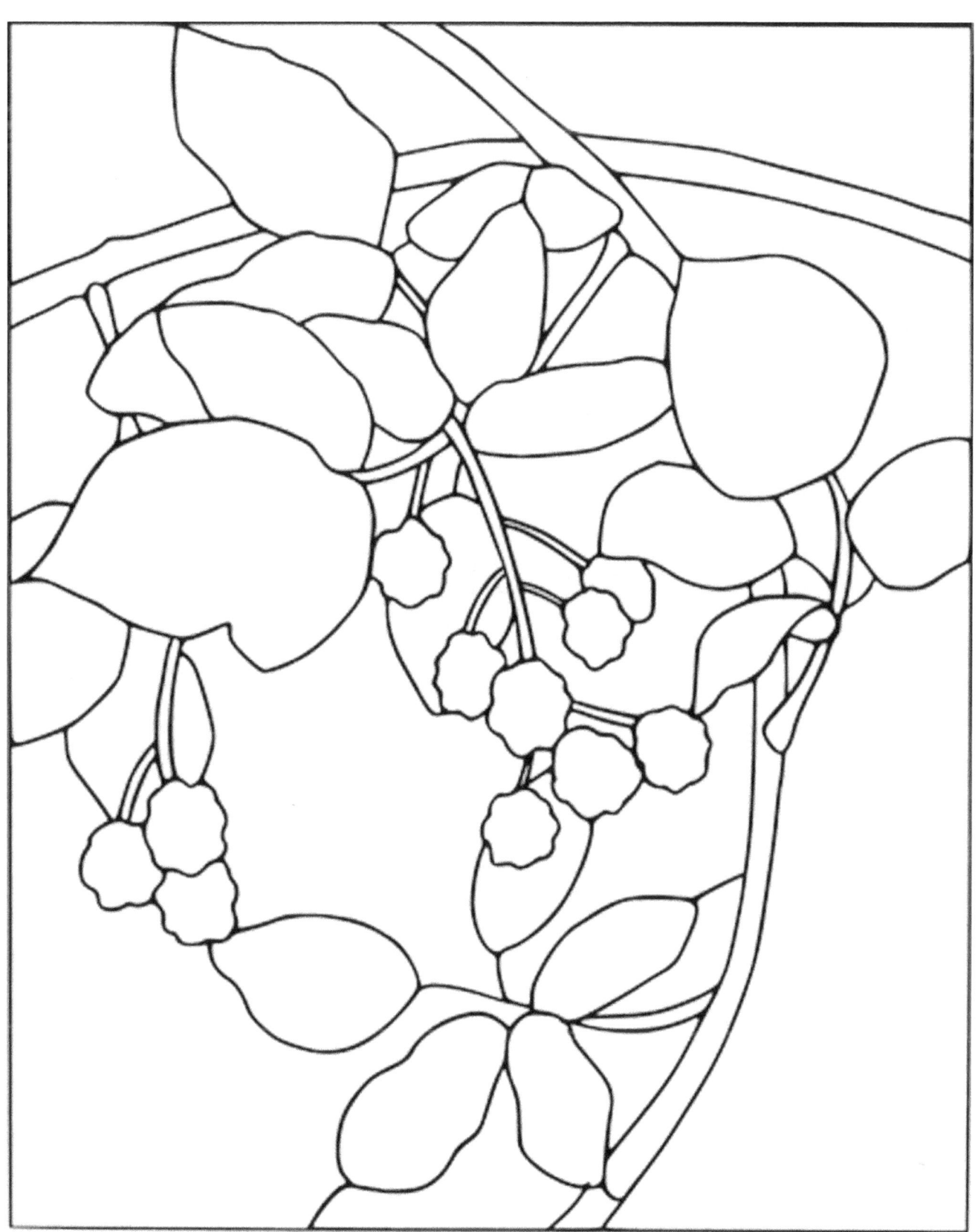

The brightness of the sun, which lights the world

The brightness of the moon and of fire – these are my Glory

From the Bhagavad Gite

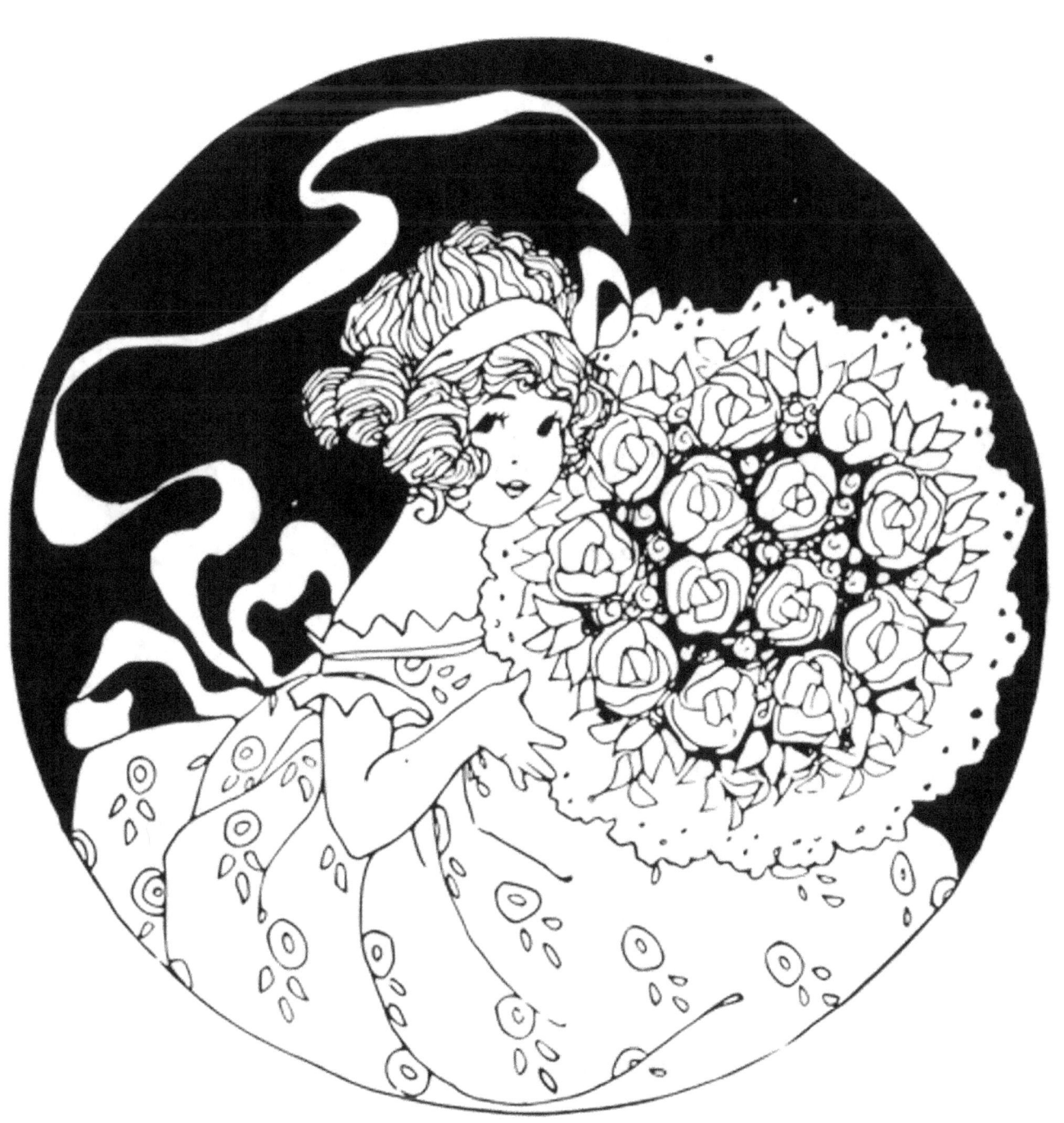

As sunlight maintains the universe, so the light of the soul maintains this material body

From the Bhagavad Gita

Please review this book

Thank you

www.ingramcontent.com/pod-product-compliance
Lightning Source LLC
Chambersburg PA
CBHW082303200526
45168CB00017B/2763